Kids who GROW their own FOOD

facts, notes and helpful hints

WRITTEN BY ANN ALMA

The author appreciates the Canada Council of the Arts
for its financial support of this project.

Canada Council   Conseil des arts
for the Arts   du Canada

1 Growing vegetables and fruits, young people. 2. Keeping chickens, young people. 3. Composting. 4. Mulching. 5. Harvesting. 6. Journaling. 7. Recipes.

Produced by:
FriesenPress
Suite 300 – 852 Fort Street
Victoria, BC, Canada V8W 1H8
www.friesenpress.com
Distributed to the trade by The Ingram Book Company

"If you want to be happy for a lifetime, plant a garden."

(Old Chinese proverb)

CONTENTS

WHO ARE THESE YOUNG GARDENERS?

All the growers live in the Kootenays in British Columbia.

Jenna is fourteen, and is Coast Saanich First Nations. She lives in the city's suburb, in front of a mountain. This year, she is growing corn.

Keira is thirteen. **Benn**, who is nine, is her brother. They live with their parents and their two horses on a forested hillside. Keira and Benn each have their own small garden plot, but they also help with the family garden.

Espoir is twelve. She lives in a city townhouse, but she's moving over the summer. That's why she is growing some vegetables in containers.

Cale is eleven. **Quinn**, his brother, is ten, The boys live on a farm in a valley. Cale and Quinn are Doukhobors. Doukhobors are of Russian descent. The family has a long tradition of having chickens and growing foods together in their large gardens.

Josie is eleven. Her house is set on a tree-covered hill. She has her own garden plots in raised beds.

Bradley is eleven. He lives on a farm in a flat, open valley. This year Bradley, who lives on a Doukhobor farm, is growing food in his own plot. He also helps his Baba with the family gardens. He is in charge of the farm's fowl.

Sage is ten. She and her sister **Enna**, who is four, live in a city house. Sage has her own garden section this year while Enna helps her grandmother in the garden and looks after some potted vegetables.

A big thank you to the great kids (and their parents) who let me follow them around as they grew food, and who so willingly answered all the questions I had for them.

I also appreciate the editorial assistance from Kathy Baker, Leah Gray and Lorna Inkster, as well as the *pyrahi* recipe from Elaine Woods.

Many thanks to Jody Dudley for all his help in setting up the desktop publishing design.

PART ONE: SPRING INTO ACTION

1 READY, SET, DIG

When evenings are still cold and dark, gardeners dream and plan. What to grow? When to start? Where to plant?

Once the frost has gone and the ground warms up, growers get to work. Like a grumpy bear after hibernation, the soil needs to be woken up and fed. The earth is a plant's food bowl and if the soil is full of good *nutrients*, the seedlings have a great place to grow big, strong and healthy.

Several years ago Keira and Benn moved into a new house on a forested hillside.

For a few years they and their parents worked hard to make a big terraced area with rock borders. They changed the silty dirt to good garden soil by adding loads of composted manure from their horses, lots of peat moss and some garden lime. Now the soil is in great shape.

THE SCOOP ON POOP

For millions of years nature has used manure to make food for plants. A seed planted in soil with a shovelful of manure mixed in will grow into a healthier plant than a seed planted in dirt without it.

Keira's horse, Licorice, demonstrates nature's cycle:

1. Composted horse manure makes the soil rich.
2. Plants grow better.
3. Licorice eats lots of good food.
4. Licorice's manure is raked into a pile and left for a year.
5. The manure gets hot enough to decompose everything Licorice ate into plant food.
6. The composted manure goes to the garden and the cycle starts all over again.

As well as composted manure—or instead of it, many gardeners dig household compost into their gardens.

Sage and Enna have a pile of household compost that is alive with fat, happy worms. They use their compost once a year, in early spring, when it has an earthy smell and the crumbly bits break easily in their hands. The more compost they use, the healthier the soil becomes.

Making compost is easy: any time ingredients are available they go on a pile or in a compost bin. While tiny *microbes* decompose everything, they give off gas that heats the compost. A good compost pile feels warm. Covering the pile heats the compost up more and it also keeps the birds away.

Good compost has more than one or two kinds of waste. Grass clippings and weeds

alone won't make compost. To make healthy compost, gardeners mix layers of fresh, green waste with layers of dry, brown waste. They cut up bigger bits. Once in a while they mix everything up and let in some fresh air.

To make good compost that heats up fast, use half to two thirds brown waste.

GARDEN SOIL

Soil comes from two things:

* Rocks that have broken down, called minerals.
* Plants and trees that have rotted, called organic matter.

Soil is part minerals and part organic matter. To check the soil, pick up a handful and squeeze it. If it runs out between your fingers it's mostly sand. If it becomes a tight ball there's a lot of clay in it. The best soil is a crumbly mixture.

How to make good compost

✔ Things to add	✘ Things not to add
Fresh, green waste: kitchen scraps tea bags and coffee grounds lawn clippings weeds farm animal manure	bones, fish, meat, grease, oil, fats and dairy products (to keep animals out.) clippings sprayed with chemicals weeds with long, creeping roots weeds with lots of seeds on them waste from pets like cats and dogs
Dry, brown waste: fall leaves, dead flowers, straw and hay sawdust pine needles some shredded cardboard newspaper, egg cartons egg shells and nut shells some garden soil and old soil from potted plants some wood ashes	plants with diseases woodchips cat litter

IF YOU FEED THE SOIL
THE SOIL WILL FEED
THE PLANTS
AND THE PLANTS
WILL FEED YOU.

It's better to keep weeds and creeping roots out of household compost.
In small compost piles their seeds and roots will not decompose enough and the gardner ends up spreading them on the garden.

2 SCRATCH AND PECK

Cale and Quinn have twenty hens and one rooster at their farm. The free-range poultry fertilize the gardens while they run around and scratch at the soil to find grass, weeds and bugs to eat. They make a big fuss when they discover a worm to snack on.

In the spring the boys rake up the chicken manure in the coop and the pen. They spread this on the garden before it is tilled.

Quinn feeds a worm to a chicken.

Every day, before dusk, the chickens return to the coop to roost. Some flap around in a box of wood ashes to get rid of any bugs that may have come off the tall weeds and settled in their feathers. The boys close the hatch to the outside pen and the door to the henhouse securely. They have to keep the poultry safe from the bears and coyotes that roam the hills at night.

In the morning the brothers feed and water the hens and gather the eggs. They sell some of the eggs and use the money for extra school activities.

The rooster tried to peck them a few times so Cale and Quinn have worked out a system. While one brother opens the hatch, calls the fowl outside and feeds them vegetable scraps, the other collects the eggs and fills the water and grain dishes.

Sometimes a chicken is still in the middle of laying her egg. The boys can tell by the slow clucking sounds the hen makes that she's not ready to get off the nest.

One early, cold spring day, a box that emits loud peeping sounds arrives at Cale and Quinn's farm. Inside are fifteen fuzzy one-day-old chicks. The babies have to stay under a heat lamp. At first the yellow balls of fluff bumble around in a large tub in the warm basement. Sadly, one chick doesn't survive. The others grow quickly on the special feed that is available to them all day long.

After a few weeks Quinn and Cale take the chicks to an old shed. The heat lamp, like an artificial mother hen, hangs over them for the first month.

The post also delivers sixty newly hatched chicks to Bradley. The older chickens on his farm wear different coloured rings on one

Quinn carries a chick to its new home.

leg. This way Bradley's family can tell a chicken's age. Older chickens stop laying enough eggs after a few years. That's why instead of producing food they then become food.

Bradley's forty Araucana chickens lay eggs with blue-green shells. He collects, cleans and sorts the eggs and sells them to neighbors, friends and teachers.

After hatching from an egg, a chick has a yolk sack inside its belly that feeds it for the first forty-eight hours. That's why newly hatched chicks can be sent to a farm by mail.

Bradley leaves one broody hen alone. She has decided to sit on a nest and hatch her own eggs.

Four duck eggs have hatched in the family's incubator. One of the ducklings is malformed and doesn't survive. Three ducklings stay under a heat lamp until they are big enough that a crow or hawk cannot carry them off. Then they can join the chickens and geese in the main coop.

Some of these birds will one day end up on the family's dinner table, so Bradley tries hard not to make the poultry into pets.

Bradley feeds his chickens every day.

Q: Why was the hawk in the henhouse?
A: It wanted to ruffle some feathers.

Q: Why did the chicken set her alarm rooster?
A: She heard that the early bird gets the worm.

3 GETTING A HEAD START

Josie has a new, portable greenhouse. For her birthday her friends gave her garden gloves, a knee pad, seeds, a *trowel* and a garden claw. Before the last of the snow has melted, Josie is ready to start.

She dreams of becoming a chef. She likes to experiment with different foods and new recipes, so she looks forward to creating some healthy, unusual dishes made with home-grown, fresh ingredients.

At a seed swap and plant fair Josie buys a variety of seeds that grow well in the local soil and climate. She gets lots of good gardening advice from the people at the fair. Some experienced gardeners even give short sessions on seed planting and seed saving. When planting seeds indoors, using good, *sterilized soil* is important. Josie buys potting soil and small, *biodegradable* pots.

Timing is also important. Seeds planted too

Some of Josie's seedlings grow too tall before the weather warms up enough to take them outside.

early grow seedlings that stretch and reach for light. They grow too tall and gangly and they flop over. That's because there aren't enough

EXTRA SEEDS

If you have extra seeds in a package, don't throw them out. Most seeds keep for several years. Write the year you bought them on the package and store it in an airtight container in the fridge or freezer. As the seeds get older, they need to be sown a little thicker in case some are too old to sprout.

hours of daylight in late winter and early spring. So, like the baby chicks, the seedlings need to be under a lamp.

There is no wind in the greenhouse. Wind encourages plants to grow thicker, stronger stems. The best seedlings, whether grown indoors at home or bought, are the ones with short, sturdy stems. Lightly tapping the seedlings at least once a day helps the stems grow stronger.

Because this is the first time she's using her greenhouse, Josie learns that not all seeds are good for starting indoors. Next year she will wait to plant carrots, peas, corn, radishes and beets right in the garden. But her tomato, pepper, cucumber, squash and pumpkin seeds do well in the warm, sunny space. They don't like cold soil or chilly nights.

Behind Josie's property, on a hillside, is an orchard. About a hundred years ago settlers planted the fruit trees that are now old and gnarled. Over the years bears have broken many branches while trying to get to the fruit at the top. Birds built nests in large holes in the trunks.

After winter is over, but before the sap starts to run through the tree and the little buds turn green, Josie heads out with the pruning shears. She cuts some of the branches off the apple and plum trees. By pruning out the dead wood, the buds on the branches that are left grow bigger and healthier. Even though these trees are old, Josie expects them to be full of blossoms and bees in a month.

The three main reasons for pruning a tree are
1. To cut out damaged, dead or diseased branches.
2. To let more air and light into the centre.
3. To give the tree a nice shape.

THE BUZZ ON BEES

Blossoms need bees, wasps, other insects and hummingbirds to pollinate them. To attract insects, flowers have beautiful colours and sweet smells.

A bee crawls into a flower to get the sweet nectar. Pollen from the blossom's male part, the anther, collects on the bee while it works. The pollen then rubs off onto the stigma, a blossom's female part. This allows a seed to grow. The seed becomes a fruit.

So, we need bees. Without bees, wasps and other insects we would not have vegetables and fruits that grow from blossoms. Of course tasting some of the sweet honey is a treat after working hard in the garden.

11

4 AND...ACTION

Planting season arrives in earnest when the days finally get longer and the soil starts to warm up. It's a time for work and excitement. After *tilling* it, many growers leave the soil bare for a few weeks. That's so they can hoe down the first crop of weeds. This gives their vegetable seeds or seedlings a head start before the next crop of weeds sprouts.

Not all seeds can be planted at the same time. Some can go into the garden as soon as the frost and snow are gone and the soil can be worked. Others shouldn't be planted until there is no more danger of sudden frosts and the soil has warmed up.

When to plant vegetables outside: What to plant:

When to plant vegetables outside:	What to plant:
As soon as the soil can be worked...	radishes, lettuce, spinach, peas
When daffodils and forsythia bloom...	radishes, lettuce, spinach, peas, onions, cabbage, first crop of beets, carrots and kale
When apple trees are in blossom...	potatoes, squashes, cucumbers, corn, beans
When peonies are in full bloom...	tomatoes, peppers, basil, corn, beans
Into early summer...	second crop of lettuce, beets, carrots, fall kale

CLIMATE AND GROWING ZONES

All countries have many climates. Climate is how much rain, sun and wind an area gets, and what the average temperatures are. Areas can be hot and dry, hot and wet, cold and dry, cold and wet and everything in between.

Areas are divided into growing zones or plant hardiness zones.

An area can also have a microclimate. For example, all the growers in this book live in zone 5, but Keira and Benn live on a drier hillside while Bradley's farm is in a wet valley. Cale and Quinn's large gardens get sun all day while Josie has raised beds in an area where trees block the sun for part of the day. Espoir and Enna can move their potted plants while Sage's garden is on a city lot surrounded by shrubs and a fence. Even in one small area, a plot may be cool and moist in the shade of a tree while only a few feet away, against a white wall, it gets almost too hot to grow vegetables.

Often seniors in your area are the real experts on gardening. They will tell you that warm weather vegetables planted in late May or early June will catch up to those that are struggling to survive in the wet, cold spring soil.

Espoir is moving over the summer. She can only grow food in containers that are light enough so she can take them with her. She starts with store-bought tomato and pepper *seedlings* and a bag of potting soil, which is already mixed so it's easier to use in containers.

After filling the big pots with soil, Espoir digs a hole in the middle of each. She soaks the seedlings thoroughly. Then, as gently as if she were lifting a baby bird from its nest, she removes a seedling pepper plant from its small, plastic pot. Loosening the soil a little without damaging the roots, she sets each seedling in a hole and firms the soil around it.

Espoir plants one pepper plant in a small 6-inch (15 cm.) pot, one in a larger 9-inch (23 cm.) pot, and two seedlings together in a 9-inch pot as an experiment. She wants to see which ones will grow the most peppers. The tomato seedling goes into the largest pot. Tomatoes need lots of space because the roots don't like to be crowded.

Before moving her greenhouse seedlings into the garden, Josie hardens them off. She puts them outside a little longer each day. At first she shelters the plants from too much sunlight and wind, but after five days the seedlings can stay outside. They are ready to be *transplanted* into the garden beds.

One of Josie's vegetable beds.

Because of unusually cold, wet spring weather and sudden late frosts, some of the seedlings don't survive. Still, Josie has enough time to plant new seeds.

On a cloudy afternoon Josie buys a few extra tomato seedlings in small, plastic containers. She waters them and sets them out on the deck. While she is at school the next day, the weather clears. Exposed on the open deck, in the full sun, the seedlings suffer. The thin, black plastic pots absorb heat and the sun starts to cook the tiny seedlings' roots.

As soon as she gets home, Josie waters her seedlings and transplants them into one of her raised beds. She feeds each tomato a little gardening lime because tomatoes love lime. Although some of the leaves wilt, the plants survive.

GANGLY TOMATOES
If a tomato seedling has a tall, skinny stem, plant it far enough into the soil so that only the top half of the plant sticks out. The buried stem part will grow roots. Even a side shoot cut off the tomato plant and put in a jar of water grows roots in a few weeks. Growing a new plant from a cutting is called propagating.

Enna has a cherry tomato plant in a pot. For a new, young gardener it's simpler to start with a potted plant. She also plants beans with her grandmother.

Q: Why did the little tomato plant pout?
A: It didn't want to go to bed yet.

A long time ago people thought tomatoes were poisonous fruits that would kill you if you ate them.
They grew them as flowers.
The shiny, red fruits look attractive in any flower bed.

SPROUTING SEEDS

Seeds are unborn baby plants. When conditions are right, they sprout. The food for the baby is inside the seed. All it needs is water. The beans in these pictures show a baby bean sprouting.

Most gardeners plant some potatoes, which are easy to grow. This helps to break up the soil in a new garden.

Sprouting potatoes.

When Sage plants potatoes she cuts each one into pieces, making sure that every section has at least one eye. She sets the chunks of potato in holes a few inches deep and forms little hills of soil over them. Each eye will grow into a plant.

Sage plants the seeds of all the vegetables she will need to cook one complete vegetarian meal of soup, salad and pumpkin pie for her family. She covers her small plot with *Reemay Cloth*. The thin garden fabric lets in light and water while it warms the soil. In this case, it also keeps a

Q: What did the big seed say to the little seed?
A: Don't pout., Sprout.

neighborhood cat from digging in the loose earth. Sage leaves the cloth on until the seedlings are big enough to fend for themselves.

Potatoes have many eyes.

Q: Why did the chunk of potato hide?
A: It wanted to be a private eye.

Bradley is the first to eat fresh spring *produce*. His Baba has had asparagus roots in her garden for years. As soon as the weather warms, green tips shoot out of the soil. While Bradley plants seeds in rows, he can almost see the asparagus getting taller. When the sun shines, asparagus can grow as much as 4 inches (10 cm.) a day. What comes up one morning is ready to be eaten by the next afternoon.

Not long after the asparagus pop up, early radishes and other garden greens are ready. Grazing, that means picking and

Keira and Benn try their sweet banana peppers.

tasting a leaf here and there, is part of the fun of growing foods.

Mix radish seeds in with beet and carrot seeds. Radishes grow very fast. When they are ready to harvest, pulling them out will leave room for the carrots or beets to spread. This way the carrots and beets can keep growing undisturbed until, when they need to be thinned, they are big enough to be eaten as baby carrots or beet greens.

Whether they plant seeds or seedlings, the growers check most days to see if anything new is happening. They water when the sun dries the soil too much. They cover their baby plants on cold spring nights. And they watch their seedlings get bigger.

To learn more about gardening, most of the kids experiment. Family members and neighbors tell them what has worked for them. Local seed stores sell the kinds of seeds that do well in their area. Seed packages have information on the back about how, when and where to plant. Some of the young growers keep a garden journal. Keeping track of how seeds do in a certain area of their garden gives them information they can use in the future.

Sage's Garden Journal

May 20

I planted my radishes about two weeks ago and they are $1\frac{1}{4}$ to $2\frac{1}{2}$ inches (3 to 6 cm.) high. They came up after about six days. I'm going to keep measuring to see how fast they grow. The potatoes and onions came up in just over a week. The potatoes range from 5 to 7 inches (13 to 18 cm.) tall. The beets just came up. They took more than a week to come up. The carrots still haven't come up.

June 17

My potatoes are huge. They are about 12 to 18 inches (30 to 45 cm.) tall. I found a few flowers on them already. That means the roots are growing new little potatoes. I planted the potatoes that we had in the basement. They were meant for eating, but they got too old to eat. So I planted them instead.

My carrots are still teeny weeny. My beans are pretty big. So are my onions. My beets are about 3 to 4 inches (8 to 10 cm.). My radishes are 5 to 6 inches (13 to 15 cm.)tall.

June 18

I thinned out my radishes last night. They were growing too close together. I pulled out some of them before they had red radishes on them and before the leaves got too prickly. Now the other radishes have more room to grow. I made a radish-green salad for my family with the ones I pulled out. I used a dressing of olive oil, balsamic vinegar and garlic powder. It was delicious.

* * * * * * *

Young Gardeners' Spring-time Advice.

Keira: "Use lots of manure. At first, weed every few days. Keep the soil loose."

Espoir: "Always make sure there are no weeds. They spread and make it hard to garden."

Cale: "Make sure you look on the back of the package for directions about how deep to plant the seeds, how much soil to put on, and how much room each seed needs to grow. Check your plants regularly when they are little. Are they wilting? What do you need to do? Fix it."

Josie: "Don't start too early, even in a greenhouse. When the seedlings are ready but the garden is too cold, your plants will die."

Bradley: "For a new gardener, start small with something easy. It makes it easier to follow along and learn from your mistakes if something goes wrong."

Sage: "Don't put potatoes where other things need room to grow. Potato plants get big and bushy. They smother other stuff. Check to see how much room each plant needs and measure the space."

Quinn: "Plant by the moon chart. My Baba always did this. Plants that grow up from the soil [like beans, peas, squashes] go in during the waxing moon. Plants that grow down [like carrots, beets, potatoes] go in during the waning moon. Also, you want to turn the soil when it's not too wet. During the dark time of the moon turn the soil over because there is less water in the soil. As the moon gets bigger there is more water in the garden. The moon is like a cup of water. The bigger the moon, the more water pours out. It fills up and empties as it gets bigger and smaller."

Benn: "Use lots of compost and manure. Work it into the soil before you plant the seeds. When the plants come up, pull out the weeds. Be careful what you pull out."

Enna: "Have a grandmother help you. She knows a lot.

Bradley (left) and Quinn fighting the weeds.

PART TWO: SUMMER SPLENDOUR

5 WEEDS, WEEDS, EVERYWHERE

During late spring and early summer, while school activities wind up, weeds start to spread like ice cream spilled in a hot wheelbarrow. The sun, rain and nutrients in the soil help the vegetables to grow, but it looks like they make the weeds spread twice as fast.

If weeds are not pulled out they use up the vegetables' space, nutrients, sunlight, air and water. The weeds' roots will take over, and soon the vegetables will get smothered. Thick weeds also encourage bugs and diseases. So the garden needs work.

At first it's difficult to tell the weeds from the vegetables. Some gardeners need help to discover which seedlings are weeds that need to come out, and which are the tiny vegetables. A good way to tell them apart is to sow the vegetables in rows.

CHEMICALS
Chemical weed killers don't just kill the weeds. They also harm useful plants, insects, birds, pets, and even people. Plants grown without chemicals— the organic way— learn to fight off insects and weeds. Over time these seeds and plants get stronger. Using chemicals over the years makes plants weaker. By eating stronger, organic foods, even if they don't look perfect, people get stronger too.

Weeding is not Cale's favorite
activity, but it needs to be done.

In early spring, Cale and Quinn pushed sticks into the soil at each end of a row. They ran strings between the sticks, making straight lines across the tilled soil. Right under the strings they dug groves as deep as each seed package suggested. In each grove they sowed one kind of vegetable before gently pushing the soil back over them.

Now that the seeds have sprouted, Quinn and Cale can easily

see which seedlings are the vegetables. They are the ones that grow in a straight line. The boys remove the string. They hoe down or pull up everything that grows between the rows of vegetables. These cleared areas make nice paths.

Bradley sowed his vegetables in straight rows as well. He followed the directions on the packages exactly. He even put the empty seed packages on sticks in front of each row. Now he has all the information he needs right at hand.

Keira and Benn keep their gardens free of weeds by using a short-handled claw. They loosen the soil, take the weed by its base, twist, jiggle and pull it out, roots and all. The looser soil lets in air, which helps the vegetables grow better.

Some weeds are very tasty. Both Bradley's family and Sage and Enna's family harvest a weed called lamb's quarters for food. They eat it raw in salads

NOTE: It's easiest to get rid of weeds when the roots are still small and the plants haven't bloomed yet. Young weedlings are good for the compost. Or, if the soil is dry, the weeds can be used on the garden paths as mulch. But once a weed has grown and its flowers have turned to seeds, those seeds spread in the garden and grow a lot more weeds the next year. Weeds that have gone to seed should not be used as mulch.

or they cook it like spinach. Sage's family eats lamb's quarters in burritos. Bradley's Baba has many uses for it. She doesn't pull these weeds out until they're at least ½ foot (15 cm) tall. Then she breaks off the roots and the thick, central stem and lightly steams the top half. She freezes the lamb's quarters for a winter supply.

In her bean garden, Josie grows Johnny jump ups, which are tiny flowers that look like miniature pansies. Josie knows not to pull the plants out but instead to pick the blooms for salads. Some other edible weeds are cress, purse lane, miner's lettuce, chickweed, and the young springtime leaves and buds of dandelions.

A Johnny jump up a day keeps the doctor away.

Never:

- eat a weed you're not absolutely sure about.
- taste a weed that grows along a road.
- pick a weed that may have been sprayed.

Eating weeds and flowers is like eating mushrooms. You MUST know what you are picking because even though some taste good, others are poisonous.

To control their weeds throughout the summer Bradley, Cale and Quinn use mulch.

Bradley spreads a thin layer of straw on the paths between his vegetables and his strawberries. Strawberries love to grow on straw. That's probably how they got their name.

Once Quinn and Cale's seedlings are a few inches tall, they cover the area between rows with a thick layer of grass clippings from the lawn. They add to that the weeds they pull up from the garden. To make sure the vegetable seedlings won't smother, they leave a few inches of bare soil between the young plants and the mulch. Each time the boys mow the lawn or weed the garden, the mulch thickens.

A well-mulched garden.

MULCH
Just the way people protect a nice wooden floor with rugs, nature provides a cover for her bare earth. Gardeners use compost, straw, peat moss, last fall's shredded leaves, grass, or a combination of those materials to give the soil a carpet of mulch. After the growing season, the mulch can be put on the compost or tilled right into the soil. This makes yummy nutrients for next year's crop of vegetables.

NEWS FLASH:
FOUR REASONS TO USE MULCH

1. Mulch keeps the temperature of the soil more even—warmer at night and cooler during the day.

2. Mulch keeps the moisture in the soil longer. Mulched areas can be watered less than half as often as bare-soil gardens. That's especially important in dry zones or during water restrictions.

3. The vegetables stay cleaner during watering and heavy rains because with mulch the mud doesn't splatter up onto the plants. And the good garden soil is not washed away.

4. Mulch keeps worms happy. These cool creatures move deeper into the soil if it gets too hot and dry for them. The hotter summer gets, the deeper worms dig, except in mulched gardens where their important work goes on in the top layer of soil.

Q.: Why did the worm stop for a rest after tunneling through the soil for hours?
A.: It was all pooped out.

BULLETIN: Under a dark, moist cover of mulch, through the soil's top layer, a creature lurks like a sly night-time detective. It hunts down and devours plant bits, *bacteria* and earth, leaving behind a trail of air tunnels and *vermicompost*. This hard-working creature is the worm, a gardener's best buddy.

When the hot sun bakes the soil, mulched roots stay cool. Most vegetables like this. But some roots prefer a drier warmth. That's why, for a few plants, instead of grass clippings, Cale and Quinn use the sturdy paper bags their chicken feed comes in. When the cucumber and squash plants are about 2 inches (5 cm)

high, the brothers cut holes in the bags and spread them on the soil around the seedlings. Around the melons, the brothers drape black garden cloth which warms the soil even more. Dark colours absorb the sun's rays. Melons are subtropical plants, so they love to soak up the heat.

Corrugated cardboard or the black and white pages of newspapers work well under a carpet of mulch. Four or five layers of newspaper will separate the seeds that may be present in the mulch and the soil those seeds want to sprout in. When those weed seeds can't grow roots into the soil they will wither and die.

Living plants cells are mostly water. If a plant gets no moisture:
1 The leaves' cells wither
2 The leaves collapse
3 The plant dies

Different plants need different amounts of moisture. **Wet-climate plants** need lots of water. **Desert plants** need small amounts of water.

Some gardeners sort their plants according to how much they need to irrigate: heavy water drinkers in one bed and dry-climate plants in another. They set up a sprinkler system for their heavy drinkers. The dry-climate plants get a soaking by hand, with either a watering can or a hose and nozzle.

Josie needs to water more often than Bradley because it rains less in her area. Josie's gardens also drain quicker because she has raised beds with sandier soil. Bradley's garden is level with the surrounding lawn and has more clay, so the soil holds the water longer.

NOTE: The best time to irrigate is in the early mornings. Using overhead sprinklers during the middle of a warm day is a waste because the sun evaporates a lot of the water before it can seep into the soil. Also, wet leaves and fruit can get sunburned. Watering in the evening means plants have to go to sleep in a bed that's wet and cold. That can give them *mildew* or mold.

Plants can get too much moisture. Vegetables in containers wilt when water stays in the trays under the pots. Just like people, plants don't like wet feet.

The tomato on the left is drowning because water collects in the tray underneath the pot.

Enna: "I'm going out to water my tomato."
Sage: "But it's raining."
Enna: "That's why I'm bringing my umbrella."

Espoir's containers have holes at the base. They also have a few small rocks mixed in with the bottom layer of soil. This lets the water drain out faster. Espoir makes sure her tomato doesn't get blight, a disease that can happen when the plant gets too wet. Blight turns the plant and the fruit black and mushy. Tomatoes like lots of water, but only on the roots. The water needs to drain fast.

It's easy for Espoir to keep her tomato happy. She leaves the pot under the overhang and waters by hand.

Bradley and his Baba grow their tomatoes in a greenhouse. They control both the heat and the moisture. Bradley waters the soil with a hose and nozzle.

For tomatoes planted in gardens, soaker hoses are great. Like long snakes, the hoses curl around the plants' roots and only make the soil wet. While the roots drink, the plants stay dry. Lots of water allows the tomatoes to grow juicier, tastier fruit.

NOTE: A good way to check if there is enough moisture in the garden is to push a shovel blade all the way down and pull it up with some soil on it. Is the deeper soil moist? Roots, the part of the plant that drinks, can go down far so water needs to go down far too. If the water just runs off the top the soil needs work. A garden with lots of worms and loose, composted soil allows water to go deeper.

8 SLUGS & BUGS

At Bradley's place, where the gardens are fenced in, the chickens, geese and ducks can leave the coop in the morning. They are on bug and slug patrol all day long.

News flash: Did you know that fierce battles go on in the gardens day and night? Bad bugs and good bugs wage war over the best bites of broccoli, the leafiest lettuce and the crunchiest cabbage.

Cale and Quinn have no fences around their garden plots. Their chickens have to stay in a large coop and outdoor pen when the garden is in full production,

otherwise they would eat the vegetables as well as the slugs and bugs. Quinn and Cale play detective throughout the summer. They

Q: Why did the chicken not eat the green caterpillar?

A: She was waiting for it to get ripe.

don't want the bugs to have a chance to multiply, so they find snails, caterpillars and leaves full of *aphids*. They feed the vegetables with lots of bugs on them to the

chickens. When the hens see one of the boys coming, they crowd around the door and cackle in anticipation.

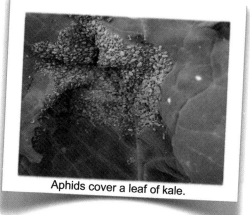

Aphids cover a leaf of kale.

Slugs and snails are *nocturnal*. When they set up camp in a well-watered vegetable patch, they hide under the mulch until after dark. That's when the feasting starts. Some growers place flat pieces of wood throughout the garden as slug traps. At dawn the slugs hide under them. In the morning, the gardeners lift up the boards, round up the slimy sleepers and move them out.

Q.: Why was the big slug annoyed?

A.: The little slug was going at a snail's pace.

Recipe for home-made organic bug spray

Cut up an onion and a clove of garlic. Boil them in a few cups of water for twenty minutes. After straining the water through a cloth ,add a few drops of cooking oil. The spray goes right onto the plants, especially on the underside of the leaves. The oil makes the water stick to the plants. This spray doesn't kill bugs, but it keeps them away because of the strong smell.

Josie tried to get rid of an annoying ant colony in one of her raised beds. She sprinkled corn meal in the area. The ants ate their fill and most bloated and died. Both spearmint and a weed called tansy have smells that ants hate, so they'll move on. Because these plants will spread, it's best to grow them in containers or remove the plants once the ants are gone.

Brassicas are members of the cabbage family, like cabbage, broccoli, kale, cauliflower and Brussels sprouts. They attract Cabbage White butterflies that lay their eggs on the underside of the brassicas' leaves. The eggs hatch into caterpillars that eat part of the leaves until they are big enough to pupate. Then they become Cabbage White butterflies too.

One way to protect newly-planted brassicas is to tuck Reemay cloth around them, leaving lots of room for the seedlings to grow big underneath. The thin white cloth lets the sun's rays and water go through, but the butterflies can't get to the brassicas.

Marigold

Cosmos

Geranium

Marigolds, geraniums, mums and cosmos give off strong smells. The colorful blooms brighten up the vegetable gardens while they discourage rather than kill pests.

Some plants have their own natural defense against bugs. Garlic, onion, chives, dill, basil and thyme give off smells insects don't like. Peppers have a waxy skin as protection.

Plants like cucumbers and squashes have hairy leaves and stems that discourage bugs from crawling around on them.

Every garden has lots of good insects. Some beetles eat bad bugs like cutworms and onion-root maggots. Some help by chewing bits of wood down so it can decay better, while others help to pollinate flowers. Ladybug beetles are not only beautiful, they also eat bad bugs, especially aphids.

Some species of wasps prey on insects. Hover flies—insects that looks like small hovering bees—do this as well. The lacewing lays eggs on the underside of leaves. The eggs hatch, and the *larvae* eat lots of aphids. They also eat other bad insects like spider mites, thrips, mealybugs and leafhoppers.

The praying mantis feasts on lots of bad bugs as well as some of the good ones. It'll even eat another praying mantis.

Q: What did the praying mantis say when she got an upset stomach?
A: . "It must be someone I ate."

None of the growers in this book use toxic *chemicals* in their gardens. Poisonous sprays kill not only the bad bugs, they kill the good ones too. By using chemicals, the balance between good and bad insects is upset. Toxic sprays can kill more of the good bugs than the bad ones. And the kids know that if they kill the good insects, they end up doing their jobs themselves. Poisonous chemicals may also kill other animals like birds, worms and bees, and they can make people sick.

The best way to discourage bad bugs and diseases and to have lots of worms and good bugs is to keep your garden healthy and to feed it well. People are happy when they're in good shape; it's the same with plants. There will always be insects and viruses, but clean, healthy gardens not only survive that damage, they thrive and produce lots of nourishing food.

A tent caterpillar can eat a lot of food in a short time.

33

9 HEALTY AND HAPPY

PLANT FOOD IS CALLED FERTILIZER

When organic matter and rocks break down, they make up soil that can have many kinds of elements in it. In most areas some elements are missing. Compost made of many different ingredients puts certain elements back into the soil. That's another reason why it's important to add compost to the soil.

Out of all of the soil's elements, three are the best known to gardeners. They are nitrogen (N), phosphorus (P), and potassium (K).

A vegetables' three main parts are:
#1   the stem and leaf; usually the green parts.
#2   the blossom or fruit; usually the showy parts.
#3   the root; the underground parts.

Each of these three parts needs its own kind of food. The green parts (#1) use N, (nitrogen). The blossom and fruit parts of the plant (#2) need P, (phosphorus). The plant's roots (#3) take up K, (potassium).

Growers know how much N, P and K are in store-bought fertilizer because it shows as numbers on the bags. The first number is N, the second is P and the third is K.

For many millions of years nature has looked after itself. Old plants and trees died, decayed and became food for young seedlings. Insects pollinated. Mature plants made seeds that dropped and made new plants. The cycle continued, on and on, and it still does.

Organic vegetable fertilizer
10-15-12
all natural
Because the P is higher, which vegetables is this fertilizer good for?

BUYING FOOD

A lot of vegetables and fruits in stores are grown to become big very fast. Produce is also grown in such a way that it can be shipped long distances. In order to do this, some growers need to use chemicals.

Farmers' markets are great places to shop for fresh, local food that's often grown organically and that is in season.

Nuts about nitrogen.

HOW ARE PEAS LIKE CHICKENS?
Peas are legumes, which means they are plants with
flowers that become pods. Legumes' roots pull nitrogen
up from deeper in the ground. Chicken manure is
loaded with nitrogen. So both pea plants and chickens
give the soil lots of nitrogen.

Quinn and Cale's garden gets lots of chicken manure, so it looks lush and green.

Some young gardeners give their leafy green vegetables extra nitrogen if the plants look pale. Others who are growing root crops, like carrots and beets, make sure there is enough potassium in the soil.

Once the plants are big enough to produce little tomatoes, Espoir adds 6-12-12 to the soil in her containers with tomatoes and peppers. This means there's more P and K in the fertilizer to give the fruits and roots some extra help. The green leaves don't get as much N because at this point Espoir doesn't need strong, big leaves on her tomato plant any more.

The fertilizer doesn't go right on the plants. The kids sprinkle it around the stem and gently work it into the soil's top layer without damaging the roots. Then they give the plants a drink of water.

The gardeners are careful about how much store-bought plant food they add to the soil. They follow the directions on the packages because more is not always better. Adding too much can be as bad as not having enough. And just the way tiny chicks don't need food for the first few days, sprouting seeds don't need to be fed. But once they are seedlings, they're like hungry teenagers.

When a gardener has been working hard, there is nothing like a nice cup of tea. Plants feel the same way. When they've put energy into growing, they'd love a cup of tea. But unlike humans, they prefer compost tea.

Jenna, who has lots of experience with growing foods, makes compost tea for her corn. A corn plant has to grow from a tiny kernel to a stalk that's taller than a human. Corn is a heavy nutrient eater and it wants to be fed often.

Jenna puts a few shovelfuls of compost into an old cotton pillow case, ties it shut and hangs it in a bucket of water. Like a tea bag, the compost steeps.

Unlike tea, the bag stays in the water for a few days. Jenna swirls the bag around once a day. After taking it out, she puts the compost back in the composter.

Because the tea is really strong and dark in colour Jenna adds water. When she pours the tea around the corn's roots she can almost hear the plants sigh with satisfaction.

Using compost tea costs nothing. It is using nature to give back to nature.

From Jenna's Journal:

I'm growing a crop of corn the way my ancestors used to grow it. I can't do it identically, but I'm trying to, as close as I can.

I always start by honouring the past. In some First Nations legends, a person who was sent by the Great Spirit brought the corn seeds. In other legends, the crow brought the kernels of corn. The crow would not be harmed, not even if it damaged the corn field. Many tribes had a seed planting ceremony to make sure the corn would be great at harvest time.

Corn is part of the Native Americans' three sisters: Corn, Beans, and Squash. The women would go to the top of a hill and plant the corn in a few circles. When it came up they would plant the beans around the outside of the corn seedlings. They planted the squash last and farthest away from the corn. On a three-ring target board, corn would be the smallest ring, squash would be the biggest ring, with beans in the middle.

These three vegetables represent how we as humans support each other.

So now I'm going to plant my corn. First I dig a 1½ inch (4 cm.) trench in the ground. That's where I put the seeds, spaced out about 5 inches (12 cm.). For fun I cover the seeds with my feet. I kick the dirt over them and pad it down with my heels. I can really get into this.

Corn takes a lot of care or it will die. I water the seeds right after I plant them. And when it gets hot, I'll water almost every day. I'll also have to weed them every week. In about three to three-and-a-half months the corn should be ready to eat.

Q: What did the corn say to the squash?
A: "Tell me a joke. I'm all ears."

Q: What did the squash say to the corn?
A: "You're so corny."

Q: What did the pollen say to the stigma?
A: . I see you're having a bad hair day.

Corn's pollen is made in the feathery tassels (the stamen) at the top of the tall plant. The pollen floats down from the tassels. It reaches the fine silky hairs (the stigma) growing out of a husk farther down the stalk. Each grain of pollen that lands on one of the hairs uses it as a path to slide into the husk and onto a tiny baby cob. That one grain of pollen then grows one kernel of corn on the cob inside the husk. Lots of pollen has to fertilize lots of stamens before the cob is full of corn kernels. Corn grows better in patches so more pollen can reach the stigma.

These two cobs of corn show how one was fertilized well while the other didn't get enough pollen.

How to keep gardens healthy

1. Rotate the vegetables from year to year. Different plants use different nutrients from the soil. If vegetables swap places every year they'll stay healthier.

2. Use buddy planting. Some plants like to grow together. Others don't.

Cabbage and onions are best buddies.

Corn likes squashes.

Plants to grow side by side :
- Beans, peas, carrots, chard, corn, squashes, potatoes, radishes, peppers, lettuce, brassicas, cucumbers, nasturtiums, basil all like each other.
- Brassicas like onions, garlic, chives, catnip, chamomile.
- Tomatoes like cucumbers, carrots, parsley, peppers, chives, thyme.
- Corn, beans and squashes go well together.
- Almost any vegetable likes to be beside marigolds.

Plants not to grow side by side :
- Beans and peas don't like garlic or onions.
- Brassicas don't like tomatoes.
- Potatoes don't like tomatoes.
- Carrots don't like dill.
- Cucumbers don't like sage.

3. Don't crowd the vegetables. Give them as much room as the seed packages tell you they need. If you buy seedlings ask the nursery owner how big the plant might get. At first the garden will look too empty, but don't be fooled: plants grow and spread. By summer, they'll use all the space the seed package suggested you give them. Thin out crowded plants, otherwise they won't be healthy. Crowded plants that are too busy trying to survive won't have time to make good fruit.

4. Make sure plants that will grow tall won't shade the ones that stay small. Put corn, sunflowers and pole beans on the north side of the garden plot. The vegetables and fruits that stay small, like strawberries, carrots and beets, do better on the south side of the garden where they get sun.

5. Grow organic. Chemicals kill more than just weeds and bad bugs.

6. Separate some of the plants that attract the same bugs, like all the brassicas. Spread them throughout the gardens. That way the bugs have a harder time finding them all and you can get rid of the bad bugs before they find the next brassicas.

7. Clean up plants with diseases like mildew, mold or blight right away so the disease can't spread. Don't even put those leaves or plants into the compost. Get rid of them in the garbage

8. Give your vegetables a health tea or fertilizer.

9. Use compost and mulch.

10. Birds help to control bugs. If you can't have chickens, ducks or geese (and even if you can have them) encourage birds to live on your property. Have nesting places for them. Set up a bird bath in the summer and give them bird seeds in the winter.

11. Respect all nature. Birds and bats eat bugs. Frogs, toads, salamanders, turtles, shrews, spiders and garter snakes do too. Snakes and worms aerate the soil. Cooperate with nature, because then your garden will be happy.

Harvesting starts in late spring or early summer. By this time, radishes, strawberries, spinach, lettuce, peas, asparagus, beet greens, baby carrots all are ready in the garden.

Cale loves his home-grown peas.

One of Josie's raised beds is full of herbs. The herbs come up year after year and give beauty, sweet smells, and a place for pollinating insects and butterflies to thrive. Josie uses her herbs in many dishes.

Both Josie and Sage have nasturtiums in containers. The seeds are big and the plants grow fast. The peppery leaves are great in sandwiches while the flowers taste like honey. The best part is that the more flowers the kids pinch off, the more flowers the nasturtiums grow. Sage picks the dead flowers as well (called deadheading) so the plant will keep blooming until the first frost arrives. When aphids settle on the plant, Sage blows them off with a blast from the garden hose.

Sage and Enna picking nasturtium seeds.

The blooms that are left on the nasturtium become seeds. Because they are big, they can easily be gathered and stored, or pickled and eaten like capers. Nasturtiums help Sage to teach her sister, Enna, about nature's cycle of seeds: seeds become plants that grow, and flowers go back to seeds that can be planted again next year.

Keira and Benn's gardens, with all that composted horse manure, are very productive. The raspberries' thick hedge is held together with posts and wire. The

straight row forms a solid border between the garden and the horse pasture. Large red raspberries are available as snacks any time of the day for the family, visitors and dogs.

Benn is the king of salads at his home. He gets all the ingredients from the family gardens, which, in July, are lettuce, spinach, cucumbers, carrots, beets, peas, chives and radishes. He picks the vegetables right before supper time so they are very

This heavy melon gets support from an old stocking.

Keira checks her cucumbers regularly.

fresh. Even the smallest and the misshapen ones taste great. He washes, cuts, grates and mixes the produce into a bowl. He adds some roasted pumpkin seeds and a dressing made with home-

43

grown herbs.

Benn and Keira's family use a support structure that allows the cucumbers to grow clean, straight and off the soil. Their tomatoes are also supported. Each tomato plant sends new shoots out of every leaf junction. These shoots suck up a lot of nutrients and they make the plants hard to manage.

Benn prunes his cherry tomatoes.

Benn doesn't want a jungle of bushy, green stems and leaves. He wants vines full of small yellow flowers that turn into lots of fruit. So he prunes off the new side shoots when they appear. Towards the end of summer he even cuts off most of the leaves. This allows for lots of light and air on the fruit while it sends all the energy into ripening the masses of little green and red cherry tomatoes.

Cale and Quinn's family have lots of tomatoes too. The plants grow in two tall, thick rows that are tied to sturdy wooden structures complete with solar-powered lamps. At night, in the shimmering light, while you walk the mulched path that resembles a bridge between two hedges, you can almost imagine the troll underfoot. Gathering big, ripe tomatoes is not only easy for the brothers, it's also fun.

USING POLES AND STAKES

The best poles and stakes are made of strong, dead wood or bamboo.

Fresh branches cut from living trees may grow roots when they are pushed onto soil that is full of nutrients and moisture. The branch then uses the vegetables' food to grow into a tree.

Wood that has been treated does not make good stakes. Whatever was used to treat the wood may leach into the soil. The plants' roots will pick it up. It may slow down the plants' growth or even kill them.

Q: How did Hansel and Gretel know the witch had changed with the times?
A: Her house was made of veggies and dip.

Josie's Garden Journal

July 1,
Today I harvested my Chinese cabbage. I left one inch of the stem to see if it would grow again. We will have the cabbage steamed tonight.

July 5,
I picked all the rhubarb and froze it. I hope I can freeze lots of stuff this year so we can eat it in the winter.
One raspberry is sort of red. So that means more will turn red soon. I have one new pepper starting to grow on the plant. Let's hope it gets big and juicy.
No cucumbers yet. Just flowers.
The Chinese cabbage is sprouting new leaves again from the stem.

July 7,
Today after a long day of boating, I came home to see a new raspberry had turned red.
I have five new cucumbers. I can't believe how one day they're yellow flowers and then the next day they're all tiny cucumbers! They feel fuzzy and prickly at the same time.
Now the peas are in action. They're growing really fast and their flowers are nice and big. They're getting taller than the support net. I have to add more net so they have somewhere to go.

July 10,
We have lots of apples and plums coming. I think that pruning did the trick. My friend came over and we made croutons with the herbs I dried a while ago (oregano, sage, parley, chives), and a salad with some of my Chinese cabbage. Top it off with a nasturtium flower and a poppy-seed dressing and you have an awesome salad.

Q: What's tall, green and wanders in the Kootenay mountains?
A: Josie's abominable snow peas.

Jenna: "I had to weed, water and watch. I say watch because the deer got into the garden. But once you see the corn growing tall you really feel proud of yourself. There isn't one feeling that can describe it. It's like a whole flow of emotions all at once; joy, pride, excitement. There is a really big sense of accomplishment."

Keira: "You know where your food is coming from. It's pesticide free. The weeding is hard, but you feel great once the food is ready to eat."

Espoir: "It's good to know that you can grow things yourself. Anyone can grow something in a pot. It's your own food so you feel proud. I love my tomatoes and peppers."

Jenna frequently checks her corn.

Cale: "You don't know what happened to the stuff you buy in the store. Store stuff gets shipped a long way and gets old and gets watered and gets older and gets watered again. I don't like vegetables from the store that much. I love my own vegetables. They're fresh so they taste better.

Josie: "You did it yourself so you know what you're eating. It has no pesticides. The fruit is tree ripened. You feel proud and it's yours."

Bradley: "It's so cool to see your own garden growing. If you grow it yourself it tastes better. Also, it's free food. It saves us money."

Sage: "I got to do everything myself so it makes me really happy. It's really amazing how it goes from a seed to something you can eat, from something not eatable to something eatable. Also, there are no pesticides. "

Quinn: "Our own food is free. It's fresh and delicious. It takes a lot of work but it makes me happy and proud."

Quinn harvests his onions.

Benn: "The hardest thing was the weeding. I pulled a lot of carrots out with the weeds. I think I planted my carrot seeds too deep. I feel proud that I can make stuff grow. It's exciting to watch all the steps and it's amazing how one tiny seed can grow such a huge pumpkin plant."

Enna: "It makes me feel happy and good."

Both Keira and the dog love raspberries.

PART THREE: FALL FAVORITES

11 TOMATOES, PEPPERS AND POTS

In the fall, gardeners keep an eye on the last of their tomatoes and peppers in case there is an early morning frost. Frost kills the tomatoes, but the fruits that ripen on the vine are full of plant sugars and ascorbic acids. This gives them the rich taste that store-bought tomatoes—usually picked and shipped green—don't have. So the growers keep the tomatoes ripening on the vine as long as possible.

Espoir had a late start, so her potted plants still show lots of blossoms and small, unripe fruits.

She brings the pots inside and places them in a warm, sunny south-facing window where the fruits will ripen.

Note: Tomatoes and peppers are easy to grow in big pots. Any kind of pots will do, from decorative hanging baskets to old bathtubs. All they need is enough root room, good soil, daily watering and holes in the bottom of the pot so the water can drain out.

Cale and Quinn's thick tomato hedges are still in full production. The sun continues to shine in the cloudless sky. The brothers check the weather forecast

every afternoon. Each day, more tomatoes ripen to their full, sweet taste. The boys have large tarps ready, and when a frost threatens, they cover the rows from dusk to dawn.

On a sunny autumn Saturday, Quinn and Cale harvest all the fruit, ripe or green. They take down and put away the solar lights and supports. The plants—cut into small bits — are left in the garden to be tilled into the soil next spring.

The brothers process a lot of ripe tomatoes. The green ones they place in boxes. They check that the tomatoes they store don't have bruises or blemishes that would make them rot.

Note: Storing Tomatoes.
Some people store tomatoes in an out-of-the-way place, in a single layer, covered with newspaper. Some stack them in many layers with or without newspaper between each layer. Others bring the whole tomato plant, stripped of leaves, into the basement where they hang the plant upside down from a beam until the green tomatoes ripen.

Q: Why did the tomato not want to turn red?

A: It was a member of the Green Party.

A TOMATO IS A TOMATO IS A TOMATO... NOT!!

There are so many different kinds of tomatoes; sometimes a gardener wonders which seeds or seedlings to buy.

HEIRLOOM:
Heirloom growers save and dry the seeds from their heirloom tomatoes in the fall. These seeds grow exactly the same kind of plant and fruit the next year. Heirloom seeds are part of the history of growing foods. Heirloom seeds are often sold at farmers' markets, seed fairs and seed swaps. They are also called heritage or open pollination seeds.

HYBRID:
Scientists mix genes from different tomatoes growing a totally new kind of tomato (a different shape or colour, a sweeter taste or disease-free plants, tomatoes that travel better to far-away stores.) The seeds from hybrids only grow this new kind of tomato once, so gardeners can't dry the hybrid seeds for next year's crop. People who grow hybrid tomatoes have to buy new seeds each year.

50

Most people eat tomatoes and peppers as vegetables,
but they are actually fruits

Vegetables have fleshy plant parts, like chard, cabbage, potatoes and onions

Fruits have seeds in them, like tomatoes, peppers, strawberries and apples.

Tomatoes and peppers are best buddies. They are planted around the same time, they both love sun and heat, and they grow well in either the garden or in pots. They are both sensitive to frost. But unlike tomatoes, peppers can't be stored in a box for a long time.

Quinn and Cale use their milder peppers fresh as they ripen. The extras they cut into strips and freeze. The hot peppers stay on the plant as long as possible so the sun can dry them.

The boys make jars of salsa with some of their produce. They process the jars in a hot-water bath. Because this seals the lids onto the glass jars, the salsa won't go bad. The family stores the jars in a cupboard for use during the winter.

Cale and Quinn's easy salsa recipe

1. Take skins off 4 to 5 pounds (2 kg) of large ripe tomatoes. If you put the tomatoes in boiling water for a few seconds and then carefully drop them into cold water the skins come off easily.
2. Take the cores out of the tomatoes and chop them up.
3. Chop up one large cooking onion.
4. Take the seeds out and chop up one green and one red pepper.

5. Chop up two, three or four hot peppers, depending on how hot you'd like the salsa to be.
6. Mince two or three cloves of garlic.
7. Put all these ingredients into a large pot.
8. Add:

   - a small can of tomato paste,
   - 1 tablespoon salt,
   - ¾ cup white vinegar,
   - 2 teaspoons paprika, and
   - ¼ cup sugar
9. Bring everything to a boil and simmer for one hour or until it has reached the thickness you like. Stir from time to time.

This makes a large batch of salsa that can be used as is or preserved in jars.

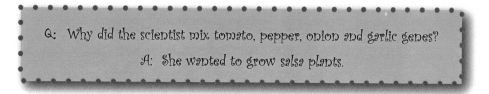

Q: Why did the scientist mix tomato, pepper, onion and garlic genes?

A: She wanted to grow salsa plants.

Benn uses the family's extra plums to make jam. He washes the jam jars and sterilizes them in

Preserving is a way of keeping food that is plentiful in one season for a time when there isn't as much available. In the olden days most families preserved by canning, pickling, drying, smoking and storing. Nowadays most people use fridges and freezers. More and more people want to eat foods that are grown close to where they live, so preserving is becoming more popular again.

the hot oven. Heat kills the bacteria that might otherwise make the jam go bad. Another reason the jars have to stay hot is that boiling jam will be poured into them, and if the jars were cold, the hot jam would break the glass. The jars' lids are boiled in water for ten minutes.

Once the halved plums are mashed in the food processor, they go into a large pot. Benn brings them to a boil while he adds sugar and some lemon juice to keep the plum mush from going brown. He also uses a package of pectin so the mush will thicken faster.

To make sure the plums don't burn to the bottom of the pot, he has to stir constantly. Rising steam shows that the liquid is evaporating.

Once the jam has thickened, he takes the pot off the stove's element and scoops the foam off the top with a spoon. Without the foam, the jam looks better in the jars.

Benn fills each jar and, after wiping the rim, closes it with a lid and a band. One after another hot jars of jam fill the counter.

While he eats the sweet plum foam on a piece of toast he listens for the "pop" of the jars' lids. This means that the jars have sealed shut and can be stored in a cupboard for a long time.

Q: What did the plum say to the cucumber?
A: "I may be in a jam, but you're in a real pickle."

The afternoon before the Winlaw fall fair, farmers, gardeners, cooks and hobbyists set up their stalls and tables. Bradley has entered twenty-one items, everything from vegetables and fruits to canned foods and eggs. He puts each registered entry on a plate at the designated table.

Bradley grew some of his produce specifically for this country fair. Over the last few years he has won many ribbons, and he hopes that again his entries will do well. However, this year's spring was unusually wet and cold at his end of the valley. As a result, Bradley is worried: His entry for the heaviest pumpkin contest is a huge disappointment. In the spring he paid the $10.00 fee for one special pumpkin seed. He planted his pumpkin in a corner of the garden. He watered it. He weeded it. He tended it. He even sang to it. Some gardeners and farmers believe that talking and singing to their plants and animals helps them grow healthy and strong.

> **PRIZE PRODUCE**
> If you remove some or all of the smaller blossoms or fruits from a plant, the few fruits that are left get all the nutrients. Those fruits will then grow bigger. Some growers use this trick with pumpkins, apples, pears, tomatoes, grapes, even with flowers. Some commercial growers use this technique a lot.

By early summer the pumpkin plant grew several big yellow flowers. After the blossoms turned into little pumpkins, Bradley—with his Baba's help—selected the best fruit and pruned off all the others. On this plant he didn't want several regular-sized pumpkins, he wanted a single *enormous* one.

Throughout the summer the pumpkin grew bigger and bigger. Then, one day, it showed a grey spot. Bradley talked to his pet plant. He sang to it. But in the end, the fruit, growing in a wet and weedy corner of the garden, didn't get enough sun. Before the competition took place, Bradley's pumpkin rotted. Now, at the fall fair, Bradley enters a much smaller back-up pumpkin and places it beside other huge ones.

He checks all his entries once more to make sure they are placed in the right categories. Like a dog owner grooming a puppy for a best pet show, Bradley flicks a bit of dried soil off a vegetable here, and rearranges an entry there. Using a little spit on the corner of his t-shirt, he rubs a tiny speck of dirt off one of

Bradley carefully tends his pumpkin plant.

the eggs. He polishes the jars of canned fruit until they glisten. He turns the big turnip to show its best side in the hall's dim light. Finally, there is nothing more to do but to go home and wait.

The next morning Bradley arrives at the fairgrounds too early. Finally the hall doors open. The participants, young and old, stream in to see what the judges decided. Bradley, rushing from table to table, discovers that, as usual, his one dozen blue-green eggs boast a first-place ribbon. So do his home-canned plums, his green bean (it's the biggest), his huge turnip, his most unusual vegetable entry (a strange-looking carrot), the cucumber and the squash. Many of his other vegetables and fruits have received second and third-place ribbons. Bradley counts and discovers that for his twenty-one entries he has received a total of eighteen ribbons.

At the pumpkin weigh-in it's no surprise that his entry is the lightest. Bradley gets a participation ribbon. Of the twenty-seven people who started this contest in early spring—mostly adult growers—only eleven entered their pumpkin. Bradley talks to the winning growers. He gets helpful tips on planting, watering and weeding. He'll have another entry next year from a pumpkin plant grown in a different location.

Still to be announced—the fair's most important contest winners: the people in each category who will get the aggregate ribbons and plaques. While everyone enjoys races, games, entertainment and food, the judges count all the ribbons to see who won the most.

By the end of the afternoon the musicians on the stage stop playing. The MC steps up to the microphone and calls everyone forward. Photographers line up. Participants nervously clasp their hands together.

Finally the overall winners are announced. After the age-eight-and-under group comes the age nine-to-twelve group. And the winner is…Bradley! He receives a wall plaque and his twentieth and fanciest ribbon of the day. Not a bad growing season after all!

CUCURBITS

Pumpkins and squashes are cucurbits. They are a family of mostly creeping hot-weather plants that produce fruit with hard shells, soft insides and lots of seeds. Their relatives are gourds and cucumbers. Cucurbits are subtropical dessert plants. They love heat. When the leaves begin to droop during hot, sunny days it doesn't mean the plant is thirsty. The leaves are simply protecting themselves from the sun's hot rays, the same way a gardener wears sun block and a hat. By evening the leaves will perk up again.

Cale and Quinn grow several kinds of cucurbits ranging from pale yellow to deep orange. They use the fruits' flesh in a variety of recipes like soup, pancakes, tarts, loaves, muffins, pies and pyrahi (pea-rah-he).

Benn's roasted pumpkin seeds recipe.

Separate and wash the seeds. Boil them for 20 minutes in water with 3 tablespoons of salt. Pour off the water and let the seeds dry. Spread 1 tablespoon melted butter, ½ tbsp. salt and 1 tbsp. olive oil on a cookie sheet.
Spread the seeds on this and roast in a 300° oven for half an hour.

Several of the young growers planted pumpkin or squash seeds. Gardeners worry about cold temperatures for some of their vegetables and fruits, but not for the pumpkins. They stay out until after the first frost. The frost kills the cucurbits' leaves while it makes the fruits sweeter and hardens the skin. That's when the bright-orange pumpkins, as showy as the red and yellow leaves on the trees, are ready to be harvested. They can be stored for months in a cool, dry, dark place. That is, if any are left after Thanksgiving and Halloween.

Benn's garden is in an open, sunny location with southerly exposure so his plants flourish. This is the first time he has grown his own pumpkins in his own garden plot. With all that composted horse manure added in the spring, Benn now has three beautiful, round pumpkins. Two of them are so big and heavy, he can hardly lift them. To make the pumpkins evenly round, and to keep them from getting too wet and muddy while they're still growing, he rests them on buckets off the ground.

Benn and Keira carve the home-grown pumpkins into jack-o-lanterns. No parts are wasted. The stringy bits go to the compost, the fleshy parts make pumpkin soup, and the seeds are roasted.

Q. Why did Benn and Keira carve pumpkins on Halloween?

A. Have you ever tried carving a big tomato?

Easy Squash Pyrahi (Squash Pockets)

The filling is best made the night before.
Wash hands. Set the oven at 390°F

1. Cut medium-sized squash in half. (Pumpkin can be used too, but it is runnier and therefore more difficult to make the first time.) Scoop the seeds out. Cover squash with tinfoil and bake for about 40 to 50 minutes or until done. (the baking time depends on the size of the squash). When baking is done, remove squash from oven and let it cool.

2. Scoop the squash out of the rind and add 2 tablespoons butter and 2 tablespoons honey.

3. Mash the squash until it's fine and put it in the fridge overnight. (or at least for several hours.)

Benn scoops the stringy parts from his Jack-O-lantern.

To make the pyrahi

1. Wash hands. Set the oven at 400.
2. Mix in a bowl together 2 eggs and 1 $\frac{1}{4}$ cups (310 ml.) sour cream.
3. In another bowl mix:
   - 2$\frac{1}{2}$ cups all-purpose flour
   - 1 tablespoon baking power
   - $\frac{1}{2}$ teaspoon baking soda
   - 1 teaspoon salt

Keira sorts the seeds from the stringy parts.

4. Grate $\frac{1}{2}$ cup <u>cold</u> butter using a grater.
5. Mix the butter into the flour. Rub the butter and flour mixture between your hands until the butter is totally mixed in and it's a fine, crumbly mixture.
6. Add the sour cream and egg to the flour and mix into a ball.
7. Spread $\frac{1}{4}$ cup of flour on the counter and put the ball of dough on this. Roll and knead the ball around in the flour until all the flour has been absorbed and the ball holds together.

8. Divide the dough in half. Roll one half of the dough into a log about 12 inches (30 cm) long.

9. Cut the log in half (6 inches/15 cm.) and then cut each half in half again. Cut each piece in three so you end up with twelve equal pieces. Do the same with the other half of the dough. You will end up with twenty-four pieces altogether.

10. Roll each piece into a little ball and roll in some flour. With a rolling pin flatten each ball into a round pancake.

11. Put a spoonful of the squash mixture on the first pancake. Dip your fingertips in flour (so they are not sticky) and take

the top end of the pancake between your two thumbs and index fingers. Pull the top of the pancake over the squash and pinch down firmly into a pleat.

12. Take the next top section of the pancake and pinch it together. Slowly close the pancake around the filling in about six or seven pleats. Make sure you do not pinch so hard that the squash moves off the pancake, but hard enough that the pancake stays closed around the filling, with a bit of the squash peeping out. For the last pinch close the pancake around the last of the squash. You will end up with a dough pocket (pyrahi) enclosing the filling.

13. Repeat numbers 11 and 12 for all twenty-four pyrahi.

14. Put the pyrahi on cookie sheets and bake for fifteen to twenty minutes or until lightly browned.

15. Eat the pyrahi with melted butter and a dollop of sour cream or yoghurt.

Doukhobors consider this everyday food. For holidays they make fancier pyrahi. Try them with different fillings, like mashed potatoes with cottage cheese or grated cheese, or green onions, mashed carrots, fried onions or peas or beets and potatoes, mashed beans, sauerkraut and potatoes.

14 WINDING UP A BUSY YEAR

One fall day Sage cooks a feast for her family. In the spring she planted her garden with this meal in mind. In the summer, above ground, first the little blossoms on the potato plants finished and then the leaves and stems died down. Underground the potatoes grew bigger. In late summer Sage dug them up and stored them. When the tops of the onions died down she dug up, dried and stored the bulbs. Now her carrots and parsley as well as Enna's beans and tomatoes are ready.

Sage and Enna's Grandmother shows the girls a shiny crystal. "Let's make vegetarian soup with this," she says.

"Soup? How can you make soup from a crystal?" Sage and Enna want to know.

"You'll see," Grandmother says. She puts the crystal into a pot of boiling water. "Of course," she adds, stirring the water, "if we had some potatoes and onions the soup would be better."

"I'll get some of my potatoes and onions." Sage cleans and chops them up while Enna stirs.

"Of course," Grandmother says, "If we had some carrots and parsley the soup would be even better."

Sage plucks fresh parsley from her garden. She pulls up a few carrots, cleans and chops them and adds them to the pot. Enna stirs.

"Of course," Grandmother says, "If we had some beans and tomatoes the soup would be even better."

Grandmother helps Enna pick some of her scarlet runner beans and ripe cherry tomatoes while Sage stirs.

They add salt, pepper and spices. Grandmother fishes her crystal out of the pot. The soup is ready.

Along with a vegetarian soup, Sage serves her family lightly steamed beet greens with vinegar, a lettuce and beet salad with goats' cheese topped with a home-made vinaigrette and home-made bread. Dessert is pumpkin pie made from part of an enormous squash the family grew.

Josie, on her final harvesting day, also cooks a celebratory meal with some of her produce. The family dines on carrots, the last of the peas, green beans, lima beans and a green salad. They all agree there is no taste as sweet as freshly dug baby potatoes cooked as soon as they come out of the ground. Only the chicken is store bought. Josie would like to have some of her own poultry, but at the moment that's not possible. Josie complements the meal with juice squeezed from their own grapes and apple pie made from some of

CORN
As soon as corn is picked their natural sugars start turning into starch. That's why corn picked and eaten right away is the sweetest, no matter what name or brand of corn it is. The older the corn in a store's bin gets, the starchier and less tasty it will be.

the many apples picked off the hundred-year-old trees.

From Jenna's Journal:

My ancestors held a Corn Testing Ceremony to make sure that the kernels were ripe. They also had a Green Corn Ceremony at the beginning of the harvest to celebrate that the first foods were ready.

When you pick the corn you have to check first to see if it's ready. You pull down the husks. If the kernels are big and yellow the corn is ready. If they're not, just close the husks back up and check again in a few days. Each cob of corn grows on its own. All of it doesn't grow at the same pace. Take your time and be patient.

When breaking the corn off of the stalk, grab the stalk with one hand and the corn with the other hand. You snap the corn off, husk and all.

I like to cook it my ancestors' way, which is really neat. You dig a 3 foot (1 meter) deep hole in the ground. You also need to have a fire outside so you can heat about twenty to thirty big rocks. You need skunk cabbage leaves, sage, and cedar branches. You put ten to fifteen hot rocks in the bottom of the hole, arrange a layer of skunk cabbage leaves on them, then a layer of cedar, then the corn.

The corn should still be covered in the husks. Then you sprinkle the sage over top of the corn. Once this is done, you reverse the way you did it before. A layer of cedar, a layer of skunk cabbage leaves, then ten to fifteen hot rocks. You cover the hole with a tarp. After you leave it for three hours, you can dig the corn back up. You have to wait five minutes before you can hold onto it and eat it.

The corn has a lot of flavour and tastes really good. Sometimes you can add fresh tobacco, only a tiny bit. It's supposed to add a bit more flavour.

You have to give thanks to Grandmother Earth before you eat. Give thanks for the earth giving you food. Remember to treat the earth with respect and not to pollute her. Don't take the earth for granted and be thankful that we still have her and everything like home-grown corn.

Cale and Quinn dig up enough potatoes to last the family throughout the

winter. They collect the tubers on a tarp, hose them clean, let them dry overnight and store them in a cold storage. This dark, cool and dry room was built years ago in such a way that, without using electricity, the temperature stays the same all year round.

Q: Why are spuds always the last to know?
A: They are kept in the dark.

The sunflowers are so tall alongside the corn stalks, they look like a forest.

Quinn and Cale hack down the sunflowers. They have to use an axe and a saw to cut the thick stalks into bits small enough to go on the compost. The seed heads are stored in a warm, dry location until the family eats the seeds. The smallest flowers are for the wild birds when the snow arrives.

As the autumn days get shorter, the trees and plants slow down before they die or go dormant. Most vegetables are annuals. At the end of the busy growing season, while the plant dies, some of the seeds can be saved for next year.

Josie's parsley is now almost two feet tall. It shows a round green flower which turns into a seed head. Josie leaves the plant in the garden so it can drop seeds for new parsley plants next year. She may also try growing some parsley over the winter, inside, in a container on a window sill.

One of Sage's lettuce plants grows a flower and then a seed head as well. The plant gets almost as tall as Sage herself.

Other plants, like dill, cilantro or mustard greens will self seed. Leaving some of those plants in the garden will assure a new volunteer crop the next year.

Cale and Quinn save some corn, pea, bean and poppy seeds for next year. They dry the seeds before storing them in labeled containers in a cold, dark place.

Besides harvesting and collecting seeds for next year's planting, fall brings clean-up jobs. Left-over roots of annual plants must be dug up and put on a new compost pile. Mulch can also become new compost, as can fall leaves. At this time some gardeners spread their old compost on the gardens and till it into the soil. Others turn the compost over, cover it, and leave it until the next spring. In colder areas some growers use leaves, straw, old mulch or compost as a warm blanket around perennials.

Cale and Quinn's, as well as

Plants that grow, bloom, go to seed and die in a one-year cycle are called annuals. Plants that grow one year, make seeds and grow one more year are called biennials. Plants that go dormant (they have a winter sleep) and that grow year after year are called perennials.

Sage admires her *bolted* lettuce plant.

Bradley's poultry, young and old, are allowed to root around in the garden soil during the shortening days. They clean up any last bits of human food, worms and bugs. These hens lay free-range eggs. With firm egg whites and orange yolks, they are as different from mass-produced eggs as butter is from margarine.

Q: Why did the free-range egg offer the mass-produced egg a tissue?
A: The factory egg looked pale and runny.

The new chicks that arrived in the spring have grown into hens. The eggs they lay are still as small as quail eggs, but they will be regular-sized in a few months. The boys collect and sell a lot of eggs these days.

One day Quinn's young rooster, after a few gargling practice runs, manages to send his first clear cock-a-doodle-doo into the air. Soon he will rule the roost while the older rooster will make a nice pot of soup. If a chicken coop has more than one rooster they will

fight each other.

All three of Bradley's geese as well as the three young ducks are still alive. It turns out that, like with the geese, one duck is a male and two are females. Bradley will let all the females sit on eggs

next spring. So his family will not yet eat duck or goose.

Lastly, the garden tools are collected and cleaned. In colder areas this needs to be done before the first snow falls. Only after the last of the equipment has been cleaned, oiled and sharpened can the young gardeners say the growing season is finished. Along with their perennial plants they are ready for a long winter's rest, knowing that nature's cycle of growth starts again next spring.

NATURE WORKS IN CYCLES.

A day has light and dark; it has morning, midday, evening and night. A year has seasons that come around again. Plants grow, decompose and become food for new seeds. Vegetation goes from seed to plant to blossom to fruit and back to seeds. Animals have cycles of birth and growth, leaving offspring and death. So, what really did come first, the chickens or the egg? The seed or the plant?
It's nature's mystery.

Q: What did the well-oiled shovel say when the rake asked it to a winter's dance?
A: "Sure, I can dig it."

Jenna: "Because you've done all the work yourself you spend more time really tasting the food. You don't gobble it down. And that way you can taste the difference. It becomes a treat instead of just another meal. It's totally satisfying."

Keira: "Next year I'll help in the family garden again, rather than having my own plot. It works better for me. The whole experience, how things grow, how having your own plot works was interesting. It's a lot of work, but it's so worth it when you don't have to buy the food and it tastes way better. You can go outside and eat whatever you want and whenever you want something."

Espoir: "It was fun. Sometimes I forgot to water. I might grow in pots again; it depends on if I start early enough. This year I started too late, so things didn't all get ready in time. I had to pick some things green and use them later. Next year I may try strawberries and potatoes in the garden again."

Cale: "It was tasty and fun. This year's harvest was better than last year's. We don't need to go shopping because we have our own grocery store right here outside the back door."

Josie: "The garden wasn't as productive this year as other years. I don't know why. Every year is different. The weather has a lot to do with it. The herbs, raspberries, potatoes and carrots were great. For some reason the zucchini wouldn't grow, so I gave up on it. Next year I am going to use some plant food. I didn't this year. Harvesting was the best part for me."

Bradley: "In the spring I couldn't wait to plant something. But this year we had cold, wet weather and it was hard to wait. Then it got so hot and I had to water more. It was good to do more of the work on my own, without my Baba's help. I learned a lot, especially about the soil's texture. It was really good. Gardening has its ups and downs. Some plants don't do well and others do great. There are always surprises. I'm pleased about how the chicks, the ducks and the geese have grown."

Sage: "It was really fun. It was hard work, but fun work. Some things I wouldn't do again, like put carrots and potatoes and beets so close together. The potatoes took over. I learned some things. It makes me feel pretty good that I can feed my family a dinner from my garden. I'm the happiest with the carrots: you can do a lot with them, like eat them raw, cooked, mashed, in soups, or make juice. The radishes were great too because they came up so quickly and were ready so soon in the spring.

 The compost is kind of gross, but it works well; it's a good thing. And that way we're not throwing away a lot of stuff, so we reduce our garbage. Compost makes our garden better because the nutrients go into the soil so the plants can eat. It's free food for plants. I'd like to garden again next year."

Quinn: "It was kind of hard to pick all the stuff at once, but it was worth it. We had good plants and food this year; it was a good year for gardening. I learned how to do more things in the garden. And I like working with the chickens. I'll do it again next year."

Benn: "I brought my pumpkins up to the house one at a time and they were so huge, I could hardly carry them. I started with little seeds like the ones I'm now scooping out of this big one. And they grew and grew into big plants that spread all over the garden. And the paths too. Now I can carve my own pumpkin that I grew. It's exciting. I'd like my own garden plot again next year. I want to grow pumpkins again."

Enna: "It's fun. I feel good and happy. I want to plant some more next year. My Grandmother taught me how to weed and how to harvest her carrots and beans. And I have a watering can so I could water. And I moved the snails and slugs away from the garden. The worms helped the plants to grow too. I like worms."

GLOSSARY

Aphid: Also called plant louse. A tiny insect that sucks juices from plants.

Bacteria: A tiny vegetable body that has only one cell. It can fertilize the soil or cause diseases.

Biodegradable: Materials that can decompose and become compost.

Bolt: A plant that *bolts* grows a flower which goes to seed.

Chemicals: Using materials in chemistry to make something new.

Larva: For some animals, a stage in that animal's life when a baby grows into a mature animal. Example: a caterpillar (the larva) grows into a butterfly. More than one larva are called larvae.

Microbe: A tiny organism that can only be seen under a microscope.

Mildew: A fungus that makes a plant go moldy.

Minerals: Broken down rocks that help to make soil.

Nocturnal: An animal that hunts for food at night.

Nutrients: Minerals that are absorbed as food by plant roots.

Organic: Food that is grown the natural way, with only sprays or treatments that are made by nature.

Pesticide: A chemical used to kill insects.

Produce: Plants that are grown by farmers and gardeners and that are used as food.

Reemay Cloth: Also called garden cloth. A very thin, white fabric that lets light and water through, but keeps the bugs off the plant.

Seedlings: Young plants that have grown from seeds, but that are not yet full-grown. They are the teenagers of the plant world.

Sterilized soil: Soil that has no bacteria and microbes in it.

Till: Plough the garden soil to get it ready for planting.

Transplant: Take a plant out of one place, like a small pot, and move it to another place, like a bigger pot or a garden.

Trowel: A garden tool that looks like a miniature shovel.

Vermicompost: Worm manure. *Vermi* means worm.

My Garden Journal

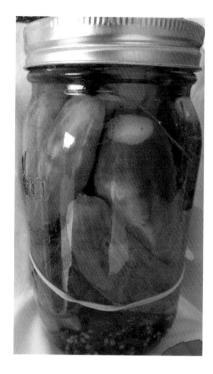

CPSIA information can be obtained
at www.ICGtesting.com
Printed in the USA
LVIW02n1543171113
361651LV00026B/617